A Walker's Guide to the Wirral Shore Way

The remains of Denhall Quay

A Walker's Guide to the

Wirral Shore Way

An historic walk along the old shoreline of the River Dee between Chester and Hoylake.

by

Carl Rogers

Mara Publications

First published in March 1994 by Mara Publications,
22 Crosland Terrace, Helsby, Warrington, Cheshire WA6 9LY

Second edition published August 1999

All enquiries regarding sales: (01928) 723744

ISBN 1 902512 05 7

British Library Cataloguing-in-publication data.
A catalogue for this book is available from the British Library.

Maps based on the 1947 Ordnance Survey 1 inch to 1 mile map.

Contents

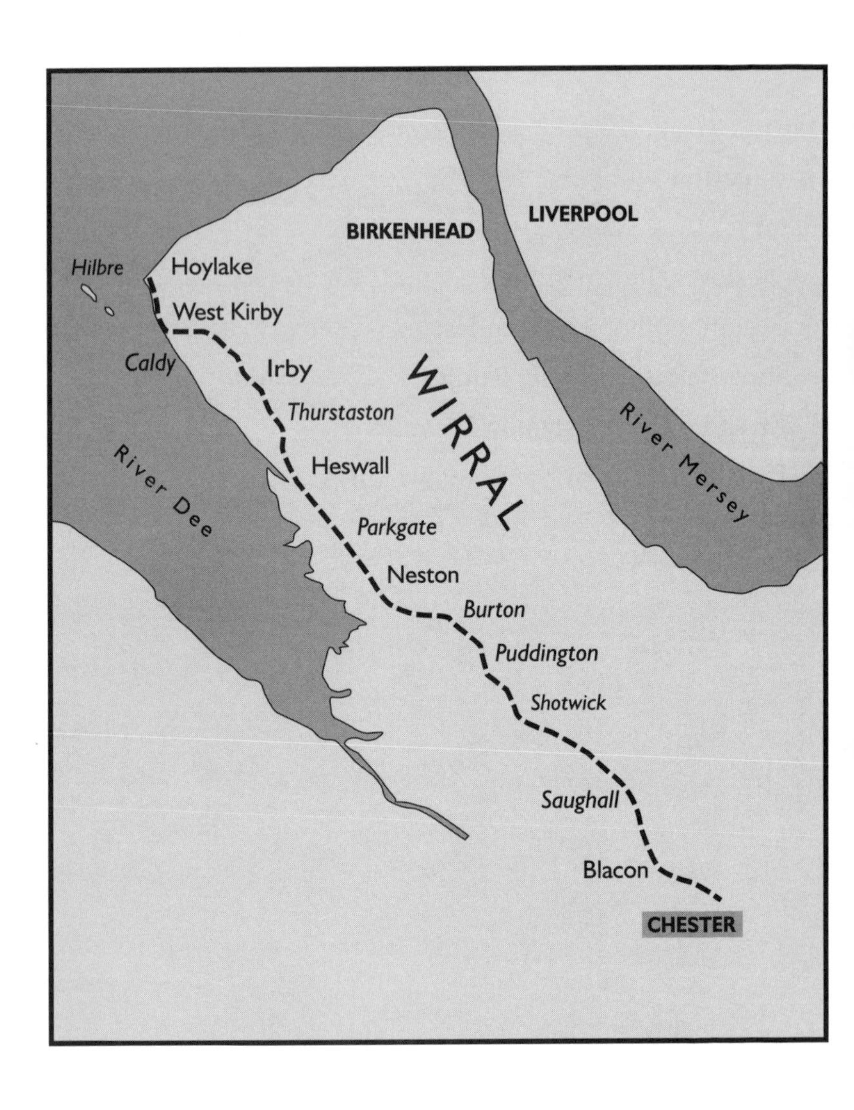
LIVERPOOL
BIRKENHEAD
Hilbre
Hoylake
West Kirby
Caldy
Irby
Thurstaston
WIRRAL
River Mersey
Heswall
River Dee
Parkgate
Neston
Burton
Puddington
Shotwick
Saughall
Blacon
CHESTER

Introduction

THE *Wirral Shore Way* is a linear footpath which links the historic city of Chester with Hoylake and Hilbre Island, situated at the mouth of the River Dee. Where possible, the walk follows the old river bank of the Dee which now lies either many miles inland, or is only occasionally visited by the tide. Along this coast, a line of small ports and anchorages were established during the Middle Ages when the River Dee began to silt up. This prevented the ships which had brought Chester a flourishing sea trade for centuries from reaching the city. The vast changes which have occurred along the Wirral coast, coupled with the failure of Chester as a seaport thus provide a theme for the walk. In addition to this link with the area's maritime history, the *Wirral Shore Way* will take you through some of Wirral's most attractive countryside and picturesque villages.

The trail is not an official waymarked route, but uses existing public rights of way or permissive paths where no right of way exists. The walking is generally easy and is, for the most part, flat and on well used footpaths. Views are often extensive, taking in the vast marshes and tidal sands of what remains of the River Dee and the Clwydian Range which guard the Welsh border. The mountains of Snowdonia and the Great Orme are sometimes visible from the northern end of the route in clear conditions.

The gentle nature of the terrain means that it can be enjoyed at any time of the year and by walkers of any ability (from grandparents to young children) and could be used as an introduction to more ambitious long distance walking. With a length of 24 miles, it could be tackled by strong walkers in one go, but is more easily completed in two sections, or as a series of shorter walks. The following chapters have been arranged with this in mind. Public transport is available from both ends of the trail and from several points along the walk. Consult local rail and bus timetables.

History

CHESTER is an ancient and historic city, its black and white buildings, medieval city walls and Roman remains have made it famous both nationally and internationally. It enjoys a year round tourist trade which attracts visitors from as far away as Japan and America; yet few if any of these visitors will leave the city with any inclination that Chester was, for several centuries, the major seaport for the northwest of Britain.

Its origins reach back to the Roman period. As far as is known it was the Romans who first realised its strategic importance, lying at the head of what was then a major tidal estuary—far larger than it is today—occupying the lowest point at which the River Dee could be bridged. The tidal waters of the Dee came right up to the city walls covering the land occupied today by the race course at the Roodee and the industrial and retail developments along Sealand Road.

Once established, the Romans used Chester as a base to further their conquest of the British tribes who occupied what is now Wales and it became the most important Roman fort in this part of Britain. Its role as a seaport began at this time; one of its main attractions being that legions stationed here could be supplied by sea. The movement of large consignments of goods was far easier by sea than by land at that time.

Until the Middle Ages a deep water channel passed very close to the city walls. This was created by a narrowing of the river just down stream from the Roodee. The great volume of tidal waters sweeping through this narrower section would have kept it clear of silt, thus allowing ships of almost any size to reach the city. Trading and supply ships from all over the Roman empire came here, their square sails being a common sight from nearby Blacon Point—a name recalling the days when it was a major landmark and perhaps even a hazard on the final approach to the port.

When the Romans left Britain, Chester seems to have endured a period of neglect and much of the old Roman town become a ruin. However, the eventual confinement to Wales of the remaining British tribes following the Battle Chester in 616 AD, put Chester in an important strategic position once again. It commanded the route into north Wales and was used extensively to launch and supply campaigns into Wales by both the Saxons and the Normans.

By the time of the Norman conquest Chester was a thriving Saxon town and is said to have been one of the last English towns to fall to the conqueror. Norman rule was not extended much beyond the present Welsh border at this time and the Norman kings dealt with the problem of the Welsh by establishing powerful barons, known as 'Marcher Lords', along the Welsh border. These ambitious men were given a free reign to attack and plunder Welsh lands in order to increase their own power.

The first of these rulers to use Chester as his base was William the Conquer's nephew Hugh D' Avranches, Earl of Chester, also known as 'Hugh Lupus'. In 1090 he launched an attack into Wales from here and reached as far as Anglesey where he built a small motte and bailey near Beaumaris before being rebuffed by the powerful Gruffydd ap Cynan. The port was used extensively in the war with Wales and numerous Norman kings will have launched their campaigns from here.

Both Henry II and King John used Chester in their wars against Owain Gwynedd and Llywelyn the Great and when Edward I finally defeated Llywelyn the Last in 1282 his success was in part due to the use of supply ships sent to Anglesey from the port here at Chester.

In the centuries that followed, Chester reached its zenith as a seaport trading internationally, but by this time its days were numbered. The Dee Estuary is wide and the sands which we see today between Wirral and Wales had begun to form around the upper reaches of the river making it difficult for large shipping to reach the city. To remedy this, a number of smaller anchorages were established down stream. The first of these was at Shotwick where a castle had been built by the Normans centuries before and facilities for shipping were already in place. From here a road linking Shotwick Park to Chester was used to reach the city. Anchorages were also established below the church at Shotwick and behind the sheltering arm of Burton Point.

Eventually shallowing of the river rendered these anchorages useless and a more substantial port was constructed in the sixteenth century at Neston. This was known as the "New Quay" and remained in use for over a century. Its remains can be seen today beyond the reach of even the highest tides isolated by miles of marsh grass and saltings. As the fortunes of the "New Quay" were in decline a new quay was being established a few miles down stream near Neston Deer Park. Parkgate is now a well known name and came into being as a replacement for the "New Quay" at Neston, which then became know as the "Old Quay".

Parkgate had only a few years to enjoy its new found prosperity when moves were underway to confine the River Dee to a 'canal' and enable what was left of the small port at Chester to carry on its dwindling trade. When this happened it put an end to the Wirral ports. Prior to the canalisation scheme, the low water channel had flowed along the Wirral side of the estuary passing beneath Burton Point and within a hundred yards or so of Parkgate's promenade. For some reason the "New Cut" was constructed on the Welsh side of the river and although it finished at Connah's Quay, allowing the river to find its former bed for the remainder of its journey, it began a gradual move away from the Wirral shore.

The line of the "New Cut" can be seen today on modern maps running in a straight line from Saltney to Connah's Quay. East of this, seawalls were built to enable reclamation of the former riverbed. Throughout the eighteenth century the land between Chester and Sealand (a rather unimaginative name for this new land) was reclaimed by the building of seawalls; the last being that between Burton Point and Connah's Quay in the late nineteenth century.

The result of this has been the transformation of miles of wild estuary into farmland; a feat which in its day must have seemed very noble. Today we tend to view such "improvement" of the natural environment very differently, but had this not taken place and the Dee had continued its role as a commercial seaway, western Wirral would no doubt have shared the same fate as the east. The decline of Chester and the Wirral ports was marked by the rise of Liverpool and Birkenhead who took most of Chester's trade.

When the last ship left Parkgate, Liverpool was already developing fast. The Dee shares a very different geography to that of its neighbour, the River Mersey. The wide mouth of the Dee enabled the build up of sands which eventually choked it, while the Mersey has a much narrower opening to the sea. As a result it can sweep itself clear of sand and silt much more easily. The port of Liverpool developed around a small tidal inlet at this narrow point near the mouth of the river. At the same time Birkenhead on the Wirral side developed rapidly from a tiny hamlet to become the largest settlement in Wirral during the nineteenth century. The grand buildings to be seen in Hamilton Square today are a direct result of the wealth and prosperity of Liverpool as a major international seaport.

Hamilton Square, Birkenhead

Chapter I

Chester to Blacon

Starting point: *Chester Cathedral.*

Distance: *3 miles*

FROM the south entrance of the cathedral (facing St Werburgh Street and with the cathedral behind you) turn left and walk through the cathedral grounds to gain

Eastgate Clock

the city walls by the Bell Tower (the modern tower adjacent to the walls).

The diocese of Chester, along with the cathedral came into existence in the sixteenth century with Henry VIII's Dissolution of the Monasteries, although the building itself is of much earlier foundation. Previously the Abbey of St Werburgh, it was founded by Hugh Lupus, the first Earl of Chester in 1092. Parts of the Norman abbey remain, but the present structure dates mainly from the fourteenth to the sixteenth century. It was extensively renovated during the nineteenth century by a number of Victorian architects.

The walls are one of Chester's most distinctive features and encircle the city centre for almost two miles. A complete circuit of the city can be made without leaving the walls. The north and east sections are built on the foundations of the Roman fort, while the south and west walls were added during the twelfth century to incorporate the Norman castle. After extensive damage during the Civil War, they were repaired in the eighteenth century when the medieval gatehouses were replaced.

Turn right along the walls and very shortly you will be standing below one of Chester's best known landmarks—Eastgate Clock.

The clock was built to commemorate Queen Victoria's Diamond Jubilee and is probably Chester's most photographed landmark. Eastgate in its present form was built in 1769 to replace the medieval gateway. Contemporary illustrations show this to have been an imposing structure flanked by two octagonal towers four storeys high. It was built in the twelfth century although parts of the structure are thought to have contained sections of the original Roman gate.

Eastgate was one of the four original gates in the walls planned by the Romans. It

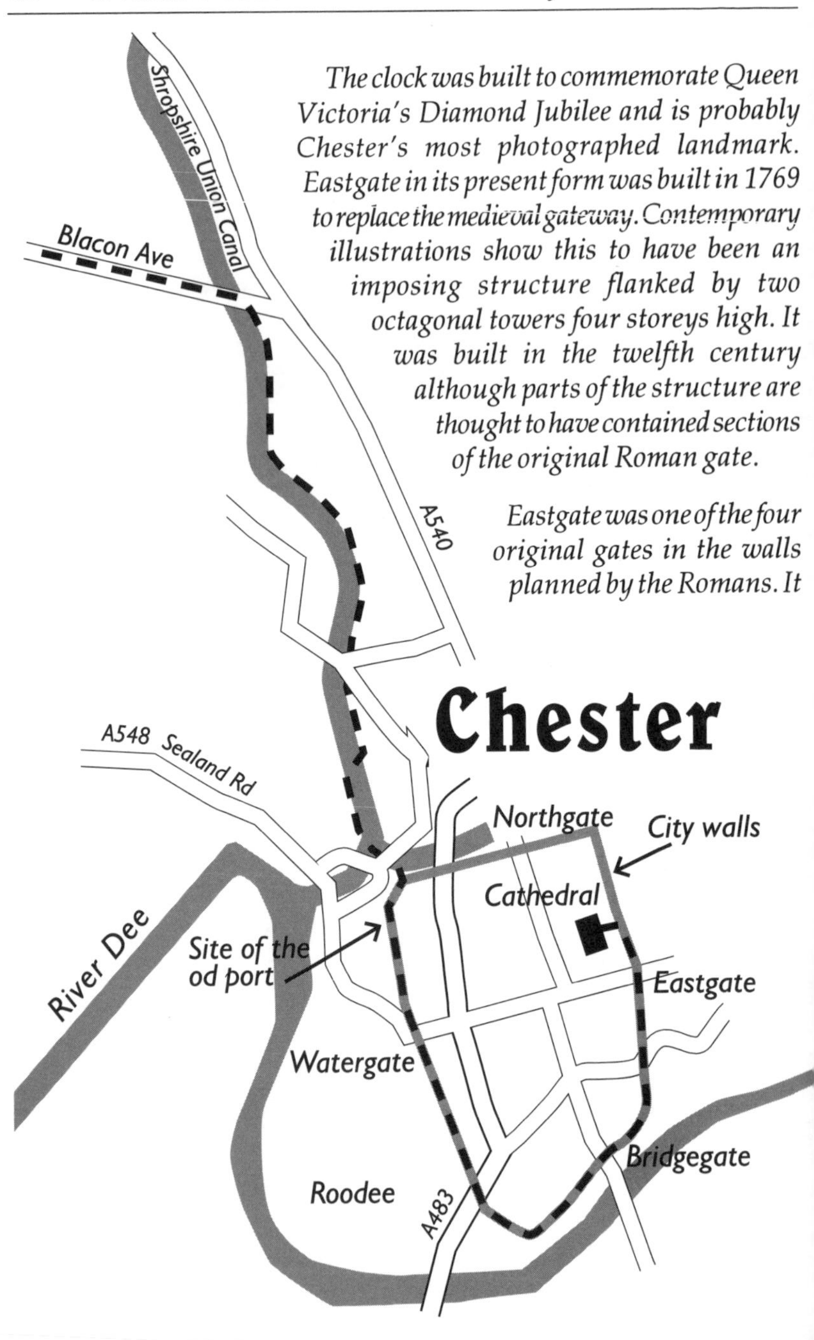

was from this gate that the road to York left the fort and for the next fifteen hundred years was the entrance used by all traffic entering the city from the east.

Continue along the walls to Newgate.

This modern entrance in the walls was built in 1938 in the style of a fourteenth century gateway as part of the new ring road system. Outside the walls you will see the partly excavated remains of the Roman amphitheatre. Although it looks quite modest from here it is in fact the largest military amphitheatre so far unearthed in Britain and is thought to have been able to seat around 8,000 spectators with outside walls rising to about 35 feet; higher than the city walls are today.

Just beyond Newgate is the public garden containing a collection of Roman stonework gathered from around the city. Of particular note is the underfloor heating system which would have been incorporated into many important buildings or the homes of prominent individuals.

Beyond Newgate the wall approaches the river then curves right towards Bridgegate.

Roman stonework near Newgate

Like Eastgate this, unfortunately, is a relatively modern structure built in 1782. During this period extensive renovations were carried out on the walls to change their character from the original purpose as a defence to a recreation facility.

The original gate at this point was the most important defence guarding the Welsh approach to the city. The Welsh were a constant threat prior to Edward I's conquest of Wales in the late thirteenth century and the river crossing was both very important and vulnerable. Early bridges were built of wood but would have been constantly washed away by high tides. Remnants of the Roman bridge can still be seen in the form of sandstone blocks downstream from the present structure. This dates in part from the fourteenth century but was not built completely from stone until the late 1500s. On the far bank a second gate and guard tower, which no longer exist gave extra protection to this important, but vulnerable crossing.

Beyond Bridgegate the walls become less distinct for a short section as you pass County Hall, headquarters of Cheshire County Council.

This section of the wall was altered in the 1830s and does not follow the line of the medieval defences. Just before this, a cast metal wall plaque marks the location of the medieval Bridgegate and gives additional information about the mills which once lined the edge of the river here.

Bear right onto the wall again immediately after County Hall and walk past Chester Castle on the right.

The original castle was founded by William the Conqueror as part of a line of fortresses to guard the Welsh Marches. The Marches were very much frontier territory and the crossing of the Dee was both vulnerable and of great strategic importance. Nothing of the original structure remains and of the medieval stone castle which replaced it, only the Agricola Tower has survived. A complex of offices and county courts sprawl around the castle mound, possibly part of the original defences built by the Normans.

Cross the road here and pick up the walls again where they back the famous racecourse.

The race ground occupies land known as the Roodee, previously an area of tidal sands. It was here during the Middle Ages that the port of Chester was situated and part of the stone quay can still be seen at the foot of the walls. Although only a few feet is visible today, the stone work continues below the ground for over fifteen feet; evidence of just how deep the river was here at one time. So what happened? Tidal estuaries are very prone to change as sands shift causing new channels to be created and filling in and choking what was previously a deep river bed. This is the case with the River Dee's low water channel which previously washed the stones of the quay here. Carrying several feet of water at low tide, very large ships were evidently able to navigate the river at high water. When the low water channel moved away, sand replaced water and the port dried out.

In the centuries that followed a line of small anchorages were built all along the western coast of Wirral where deep water could still be found. This allowed Chester's fortunes as a port to struggle on for a few more centuries, but siltation continued depriving the once thriving ports of their navigable water.

The Dee bridge

The next gate is known as the Watergate.

Watergate is the western counterpart of Eastgate and forms one of the original four gates in the city walls. Facing the river whose waters originally lapped at its feet, it gave access to the port which had existed here since Roman times. Just how important the port was to Chester before its siltation can be gauged by the fact that Chester enjoyed an international trade and was frequented by ships from all over Europe and the East. Imports included wine and spices while cheese, horses and even slaves from the Welsh wars are said to have been exports of the city.

Continue along the walls to Bonewaldesthorne's Tower.

This, unlike the gates and other structures we have seen so far is not a modern addition or replacement. It is part of the medieval defences and until the 1400s stood with its feet in the water of the river. It was built to guard the approach to the harbour and the shipping which was moored along the walls, by cutting off any landward approach. As the river began to change its course away from the walls, however, it was no longer able to do this. An additional tower was built further out on the edge of the channel and connected to Bonewaldesthorne's Tower by a spur wall 100

The Water Tower viewed from Bonewaldesthorne's Tower on the city walls

feet long. This is known as the Water Tower and can be seen today from the walls. Within 100 years the river here was also drying out leaving the tower and the port high and dry.

Continue along the wall beyond Bonewaldthorne's Tower and look for steps on the left. Leave the walls here turning right at the foot of the steps to the canal. Bear left along the towpath and pass under the road bridge. Continue along the left-hand bank of the canal until a footbridge leads over to the right-hand bank.

This bridge is known as a "Roving Bridge" and its design enabled horses to change from one side of the canal to the opposite with out being unharnessed.

Follow the tow path now for about ¾ mile. After passing under a railway bridge, leave the canal towpath at the next road bridge. Pass under the bridge then bear right up the bank to the road. Turn right now and walk along Blacon Avenue. This road cuts through the centre of Blacon passing a parade of shops on the right after about ¾ mile. Continue to Saxon Way on the right. Immediately after this, the road swings left and there is a small loop of the old road on the right. A green lane, known as Kingswood Lane, begins here.

Chapter 2

Blacon to Shotwick

Distance: *4 miles*

Follow Kingswood Lane for about 1 mile.

Kingswood Lane was an important highway in past centuries but now it is almost forgotten. Its name recalls the royal woods at Shotwick Park which it linked to Chester before continuing to the village of Shotwick. Earlier still it was known as "Saltsway" indicating the possible existence of an ancient salt merchant's route on this side of Wirral during the Middle Ages. A millennium earlier Roman legionaries may well have marched this way en-route to their outpost at Meols.

Immediately beyond the second group of buildings on the left, turn left into fields. Bear half-left through the centre of the first field to a well hidden stile in the bottom corner. Cut through the centre of the next two fields following a line of stiles before bearing left around the field edge in the third field. A stile and short entry now lead into a housing estate. Turn right at the road (The Riddings) and continue for some distance to a T junction. Turn left here and after about 40 yards bear right into Darlington Crescent. Look for Smithy Close, a short cul-de-sac on the left with a footpath at its head leading to Church Road.

Although Great Saughall is an ancient village it seems to have few tales to tell. It was too close to Chester to have been included among the Dee ports which line the old river bank further north, although the tide came to within half a mile of our present location until the reclamation schemes of the eighteenth century transformed much of the River Dee into farmland.

Its only claim to fame seems to be the unfortunate Mary Davies who was born here in the closing years of the sixteenth century and came to be known as the "Horned Woman of Cheshire". The horns, which first appeared when she was 28 years old, were said to be like a "ram's horns" and "sadly grieved the old woman especially upon the change of weather". When she shed them, which happened every three to five years, they became prized curiosities and one is even said to have been presented to the King of France.

Turn right and after about 40 yards, cross the road where a sign indicates a footpath which passes between gardens before cutting through the centre of a large field. Beyond a belt of trees, continue straight ahead to a stile and footbridge over a stream. Bear left here and follow the "Permissive Footpath" through a small wood with a stream on the left.

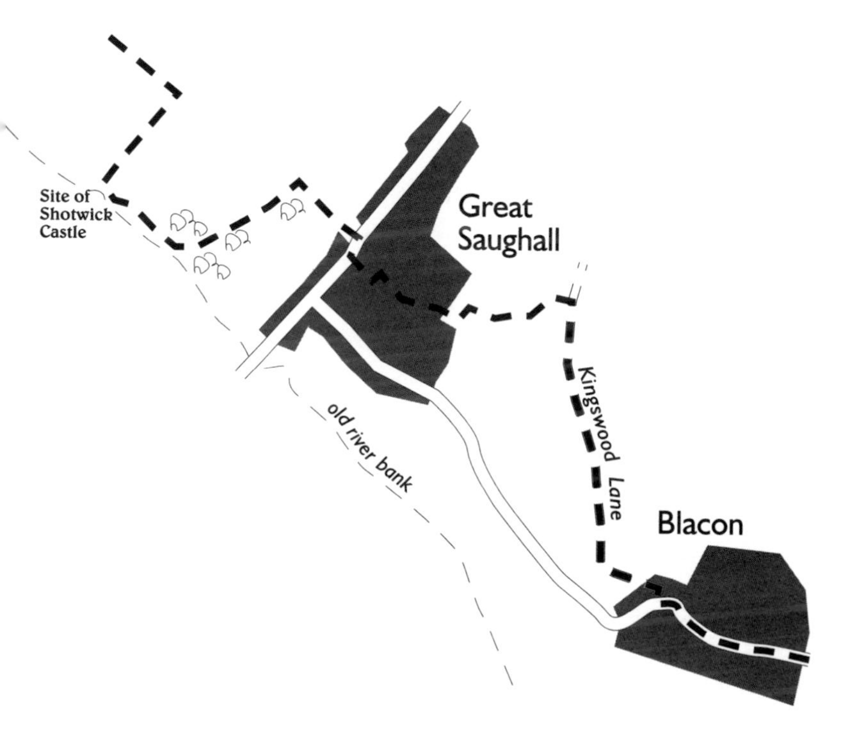

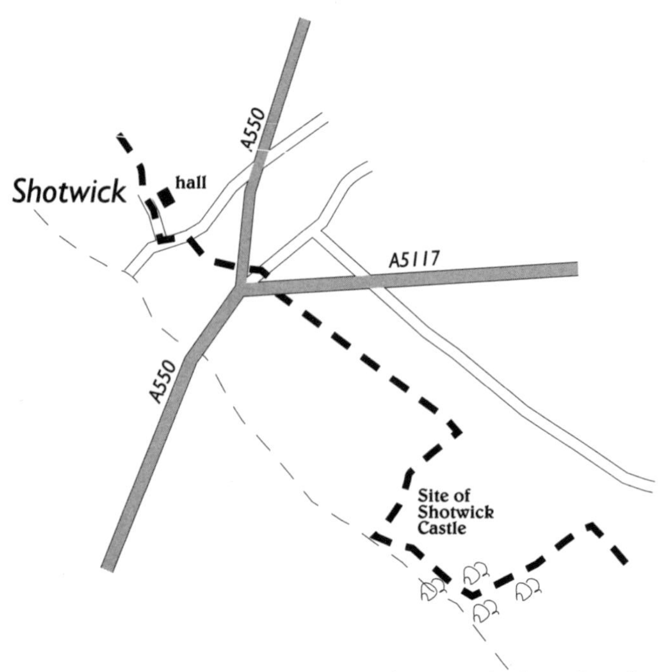

This section of footpath is part of a permissive circular route taking in the site of Shotwick Castle.

Leave the woods by means of a footbridge on the left and continue beside the stream. At the bottom of the field bear right over a stile and, staying beside the stream, make your way into Dingle Wood. At a T junction above the steep coastal step, turn right, cross the stream by a footbridge and make your way up a flight of steps.

This steep slope marks the position of the old coastline and, until the reclamation schemes of the eighteenth century, the view from here would have been much like that from the cliffs above the beach at Thurstaston. Earlier still, sea going ships would have passed within 200 or 300 yards of here en-route to the port at Chester.

Continue on the obvious footpath through the woods with fields on the right until you enter fields by the earthworks of Shotwick Castle, turning right after you have crossed the stile.

These earthworks, which also stand on the edge of the old shoreline, are all that now remain of Shotwick Castle, built to defend the English-Welsh border during the early medieval period. Remnants of the stone walls, which stood until the seventeenth century, have all been removed now and probably found their way into local buildings.

The castle is thought to have been built by Hugh Lupus, the first Norman Earl of Chester and later used by the English kings during their wars with the Welsh and Irish in the twelfth and thirteenth centuries. Henry II led an army against Wales in 1156 from Wirral and may well have retreated to Shotwick 11 years later following his defeat on the Berwyn Mountains. In the following century both Henry III and Edward I passed through Shotwick on their way to conquests in Wales and Ireland and almost certainly stayed at the castle.

By the end of the thirteenth century the death of Prince Llywellyn led to peace with the Welsh and the castle was allowed to fall into ruins.

Continue beside the earthworks and turn right over a stile following the path along field edges once more. At a signpost ("Public Footpath") turn left and follow the footpath along field edges to the busy A5117. Take care not to miss a stile and footbridge on the right about half way along the path where a change is made to the right-hand side of the hedge.

Cross the road opposite farm buildings and look for a stile behind the large road sign. Cut through a small field to a stile and lane. Turn left here then immediately right over a stile (signposted "Shotwick") and cut through a second small field (keeping left) to a stile which leads through metal railings to the A550. Opposite, a stile and sign indicate the continuation of the field path to "Shotwick". Continue straight through the field (aiming to the right of the church tower) and turn right through a gate in the corner. Immediately on the left, a second gate leads into a sloping field; descend the field to a footbridge over a stream and rise to Shotwick Lane. Turn left now and follow the lane to Shotwick Church.

Chapter 3

Shotwick to Parkgate

Distance: 6 miles

THIS *quiet hamlet, now bypassed by traffic on the busy Welsh road lies almost forgotten, yet for centuries it stood on one of the main routes from Wirral to North Wales. Before the River Dee around Sealand was reclaimed, a tidal road ran from the lane beside the church across the estuary to Flint.*

Earlier still, an anchorage is thought to have existed here in addition to the one at Shotwick Castle. During the Middle Ages several armies sailed from both here and Shotwick Castle to battles in Ireland and North Wales, among them the famous Wirral archers who practised their skills in the fields below the church. These fields are named on old maps as 'The Butts', while grooves to be seen inside the church porch are said to have been caused by the sharpening of their arrows. In later years, anchorages were established down stream at Burton Point, Neston and Parkgate as shallowing of the river continued.

Today much of the River Dee has become dry land, even the wild marshes have disappeared. In their place lie fields, hedges, cattle and sheep, and in more recent years, the monstrous buildings of the steel industry at Shotton. The only clue to earlier events is the nearby coastal step below the church and the almost artificially flat land between here and North Wales.

With the tidal road across the marshes no longer in use, Shotwick lies frozen in time. Most of the attractive old buildings date from the seventeenth century although one of the oldest is probably Greyhound

Farm, previously the Greyhound Inn. It was here in 1750 that three Irish labourers were arrested for beating and killing a fellow traveller on the nearby Chester Road. They were detained over night at Shotwick before being sent to jail at Chester Castle the next day. Two were found guilty, hanged at Boughton and their bodies "hung up in irons near Two Mills on the Heath, in the road to Parkgate". Today Gibbet Mill, which was built shortly after, marks the spot where they hung.

Shotwick Church

Retrace your steps from the church and turn left into the cul-de-sac leading to Shotwick Hall.

The hall was built in 1662 in the late Elizabethan style by Joseph Hockenhull as a replacement for the ancient manor house. In the fields to the left, a tree covered mound surrounded by the remnants of a moat are all that remain of the ancient building. The Hockenhulls held Shotwick from the time of Edward I.

Beyond the hall turn left onto a track signposted, "Puddington". Follow the track to a gate and continue along field edges. After the third gate turn right along the field edge, then bear diagonally-left through the centre of the field. Pass to the left of a pond and aim for the corner of the field with a house on the right and a farm on the left. Bear left along the field edge then cut through the centre of the field to a farm track. Turn left here and follow Chapel House Lane to a T junction.

Turn left and continue a short distance to Puddington. As you enter the village turn left between houses (indicated by a footpath sign) and follow the path, first along a short access road, then bear right onto an enclosed footpath with Puddington Old Hall to your left. At the road continue straight ahead beside the barn (sign) and join a farm track. Follow the track to Puddington Lane.

The hall, built in 1490 has been greatly altered over the centuries and as a result little of the original building remains, although traces of the moat can still be seen. Of particular note are the remains of a dovecote built at a time when fresh winter meat was hard to come by. The keeping of pigeons in this way was a guarded privilege among the gentry and this dovecote is one of only two in Wirral, the other being at Gayton.

For over 500 years the manor was held by the Massey family, famed for their love of battle. Various members of this ancient family distinguished themselves fighting on both foreign and English soil. A tale of particular note concerns William Massey, who, in 1715 at the age of 60 joined the Pretender's forces at Preston. When they were overwhelmed by Royalists and surrendered, William fled to Puddington. He rode nonstop to Speke where he forced his exhausted steed across the Mersey almost at its widest

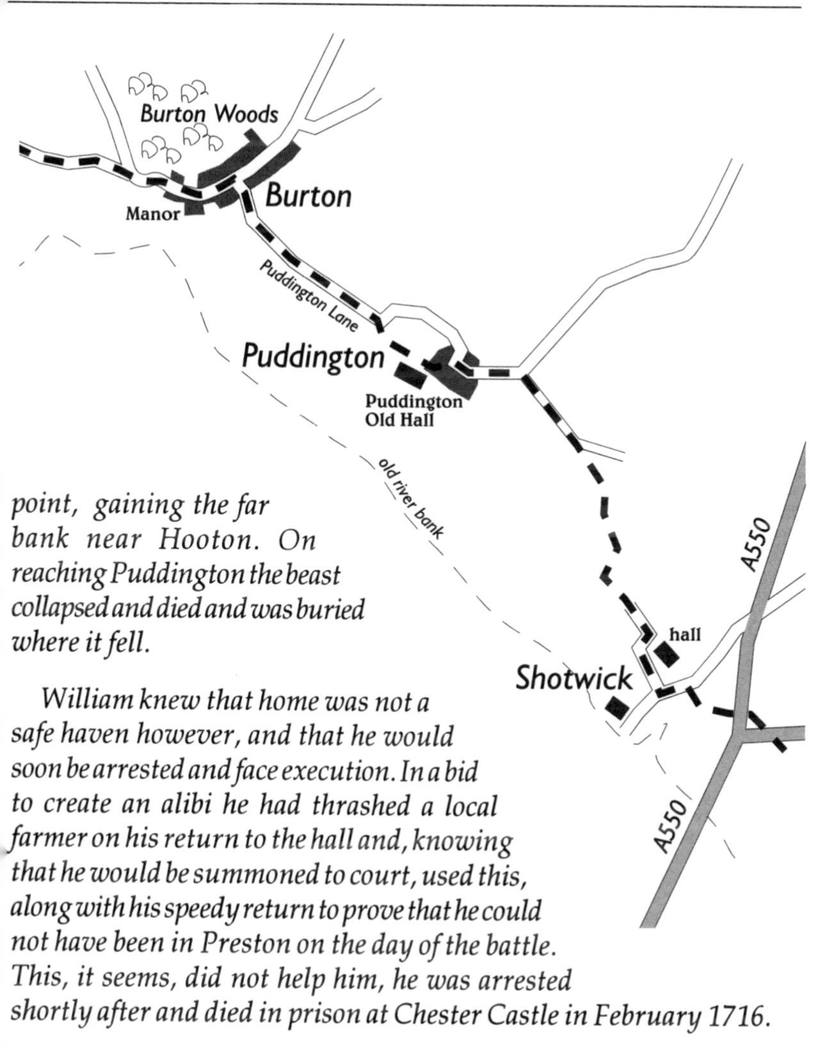

point, gaining the far bank near Hooton. On reaching Puddington the beast collapsed and died and was buried where it fell.

William knew that home was not a safe haven however, and that he would soon be arrested and face execution. In a bid to create an alibi he had thrashed a local farmer on his return to the hall and, knowing that he would be summoned to court, used this, along with his speedy return to prove that he could not have been in Preston on the day of the battle. This, it seems, did not help him, he was arrested shortly after and died in prison at Chester Castle in February 1716.

Bear left at Puddington Lane and continue to Burton turning left into the village.

This is one of the most attractive villages in Wirral and the impression given is that it has remained as a sleepy undisturbed backwater for centuries. In fact, this is far from the truth. Like many villages along this coast, it enjoyed a brief period of prosperity as a seaport and has seen the busy movement of both exotic foreign goods and large armies through its main street.

Burton took over from Shotwick as a port when the River Dee began to silt up towards the end of the thirteenth century. Burton Point, which protrudes into the estuary below the village, provided an ideal location for an anchorage offering shelter from northwesterly gales. It was from here that Cheshire archers sailed to Ireland to fight for Richard II in the fourteenth century. By the middle of the following century it had developed into an international port handling goods from as far away as Spain. By this time its days were numbered however, and within a hundred years the New Quay had been built at Neston as the river became too shallow for larger vessels.

Today Burton Point is surrounded by farmland and lies beyond the reach of even the highest tides. Of the one-time port there is no sign, although there are earthworks here, possibly of Saxon origin which may have given Burton its name (from the Saxon "burh" *meaning stronghold or fortified place and* "tun" *meaning farmstead or village).*

As you leave Burton bear left into Station Road and follow the lane down to the old shoreline at Denhall.

Thatched cottages at Burton

Here at last you begin to sense that the sea is not too distant; that the vast treeless expanse before you is not completely dry land. The old coastline is clearly visible now and there are even pockets of sand here and there recalling the fine sandy beaches of earlier years. Although there is a feeling of deterioration, as if the best has been and gone, the marshes are far from lifeless and offer a valuable habitat of national importance to the many species of wild fowl which winter here each year. In 1979, 5,000 acres of Burton Marsh were purchased from the British Steel Corporation by the R.S.P.B to ensure its future conservation.

Where the lane turns sharp right continue straight ahead along the marsh edge for about 1 mile, signposted "Public Footpath Quayside 1".

Just before the Harp Inn you will see the remains of Denhall Quay on the left. It was used primarily to ship coal, brought from the nearby Wirral Colliery, to Ireland until the channel became too shallow for boats to dock here. The quay is quite well preserved and many of the large stone blocks are still in place.

Further along the coast lie the spoil heaps of the Wirral Colliery which closed in 1928 after operating for 175 years. Here men and boys toiled in wet and dirty conditions to bring poor quality coal to the surface from almost two miles beneath the estuary. The mines were so plagued by water that coal was transported along "canals" or partly flooded shafts in small boats before being hauled to the surface by hand.

The path continues along the marsh edge to the remains of the Old Quay, once one of the most important ports on the Wirral coast.

Note: Between Marshlands Road and the Old Quay there is no public right of way although the path along the marsh edge is well walked and there appears to be no access problem. Should the situation change, walkers are reminded that they have no legal right to walk here, the land owners wishes should therefore be respected.

As we have already learned, Chester began to lose its sea trade in the thirteenth century because of "the abundance of sands which had choked the creek". The merchants of Chester were alarmed by this and realised that something had to be done if they were to keep hold of their valuable trade. A number of small anchorages were established down stream at Burton and Shotwick as we have already seen, but by the sixteenth century these too had become choked. The "New Quay", as it was then called, was built beside a deep channel at Neston known as "Lightfoot's Pool" around 1550. It enjoyed a brief period of prosperity before suffering the same fate as Chester, Burton and Shotwick and was replaced by a new port at Parkgate. From then on it became known as the "Old Quay" and gradually fell into ruins.

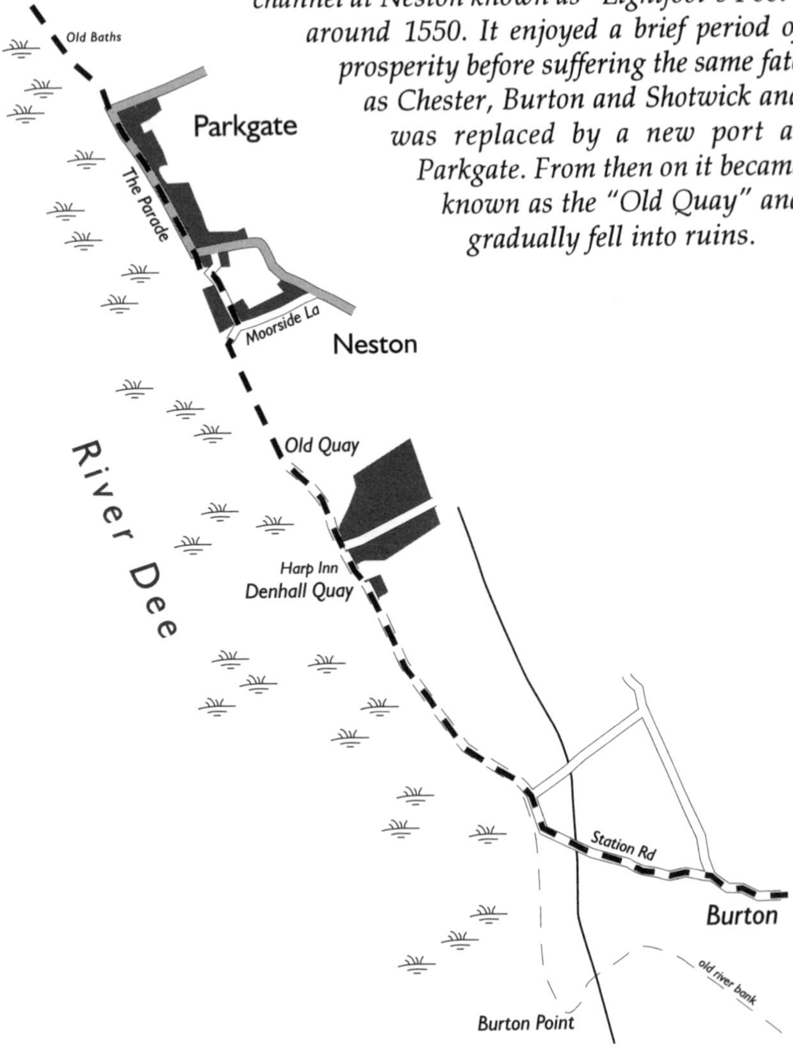

The remains of Denhall Quay

Beyond the Old Quay continue along the marsh edge for about ½ mile before bearing right by bungalows. Turn left into Manorial Road and at the end of the road join a short footpath signposted, "Public Footpath The Parade ¼". This leads to a rough access road. Continue straight ahead here and, where the road bears right, turn left onto a narrow footpath which leads to the marsh edge once more. Turn right now and continue along Parkgate's old sea front (The Parade).

Chapter 4

Parkgate to Thurstaston

Distance: *5½ miles*

IT is over half a century since the sea finally abandoned Parkgate leaving the attractive cottages to look out onto acres of marsh grass instead of bright yellow sand. It is perhaps hard to imagine when we look out onto these marshes just how much this landscape has changed in the last three centuries.

In its heyday Parkgate was a bustling seaport of national importance. This was partly due to the Dublin Packet service which ran on a demand basis for over 70 years with many famous passengers, among them Handel and John Wesley, making the sometimes hazardous crossing.

The Parade, Parkgate

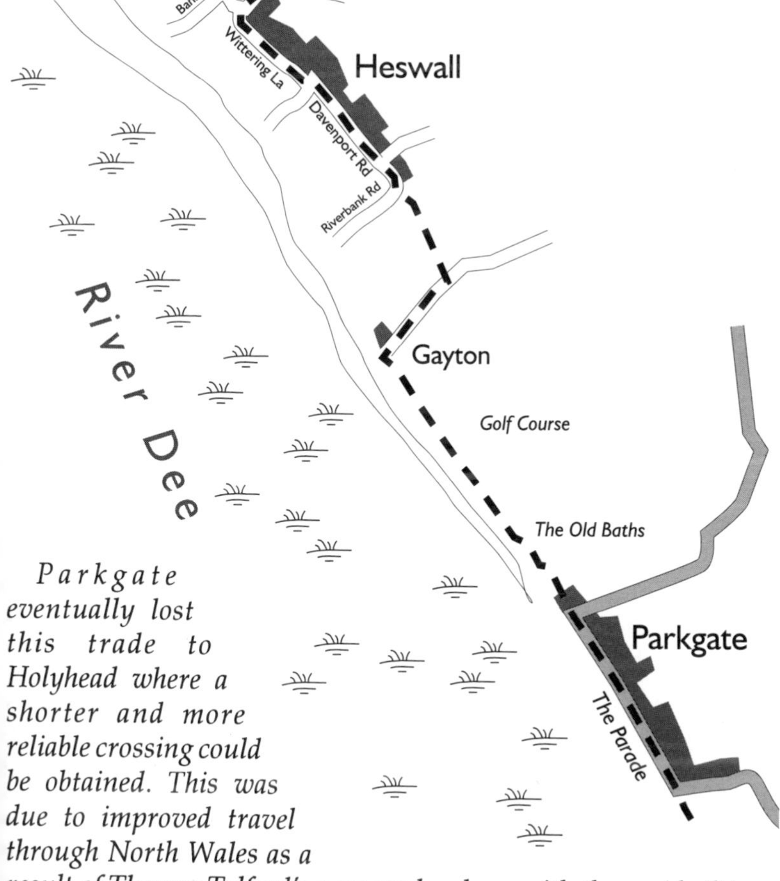

Parkgate eventually lost this trade to Holyhead where a shorter and more reliable crossing could be obtained. This was due to improved travel through North Wales as a result of Thomas Telford's new roads, along with the rapid silting of the River Dee which robbed Parkgate of its navigable water. The last boat to land passengers here was in 1811.

This was not the end of Parkgate's prosperity however. The sands which had clogged the channel now attracted a new kind of visitor, the sea bather. Throughout the early decades of the nineteenth century Parkgate was "much resorted to by the gay and fashionable world". The coming of the railways in later years took many of these visitors to other resorts but locals continued to bathe here until the 1940s when marsh grass finally took over.

Today you can barely see the sea from here, except on very rare occasions, however, we need only reflect on the fate of the more prosperous ports, such as Birkenhead and Liverpool, who inherited much of Parkgate's trade, to see what might have been.

At the northern end of The Parade the road bears sharp right. Continue straight ahead here to the Old Baths car park before following the footpath along the marsh edge to Gayton.

Like Parkgate the sea is a seldom visitor to the old shoreline here although for nearly 600 years a ferry regularly crossed the estuary to Flintshire. The last ferry house still stands and is now called Gayton Cottage.

Beyond Gayton there is no shoreline footpath so we must turn away from the marshes and join the Wirral Way for a while. Bear right into the lane then turn left onto the Wirral Way after 500 yards or so.

After a short stretch on the Wirral Way bear left by houses and at Riverbank Road turn right. Follow Riverbank Road, which shortly runs into Davenport Road and at the Wirral Country Park sign bear left into Wittering Lane.

At the end of the lane bear right over the Wirral Way and follow Delavor Road for about 200 yards, before turning left into Pipers Lane. Almost immediately, turn right into Bush Way and bear left into Heswall Dales Local Nature Reserve.

Follow the obvious bridleway marked with arrows and contained here and there by wooden fencing. Keep right at a fork and after some distance bear right onto a track by Dale Farm. Follow the track to Oldfield Road, turn left, and at a crossroads continue straight ahead to Oldfield Hall, now a farmhouse.

It was at this old manor house that Sir Rowland Stanley, one of the most celebrated Cheshire knights of Queen Elizabeth's reign, spent his remaining years. An inscription above the door reads "R 1604 S" indicating a ten year stay. He died in 1614 at the ripe old age of 96, quite an achievement, both for the period in which he lived and the occupation which he had chosen.

Keep to the right of the farm and follow the signed footpath which runs along the top of the hillside towards Thurstaston church.

Below us, the green marshes have at last been replaced by fine yellow sands giving an impression of what much of the estuary looked like until about 200 years ago. Within decades this too will have disappeared beneath the spreading green carpet which has made such rapid progress along this coast.

Although this is a natural process, man gave nature a helping hand here when he diverted the River Dee into the New Cut on the Welsh side of the estuary in the eighteenth century. This had the effect of

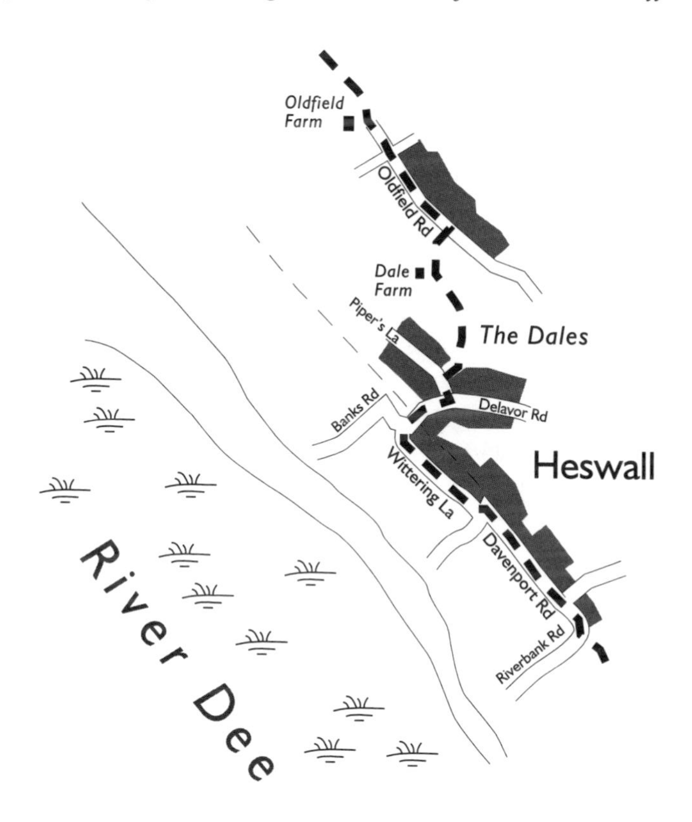

forcing the main deep water channel (which enabled ports like Parkgate and Neston to take sea going vessels) over to the Welsh side, thus allowing sands along the Wirral coast to build up more rapidly. In addition, a particularly hardy and fast spreading species of marsh grass was introduced when the estuary around Sealand was reclaimed. This colonised the sands at a tremendous rate robbing resorts like Parkgate of its once famous beach.

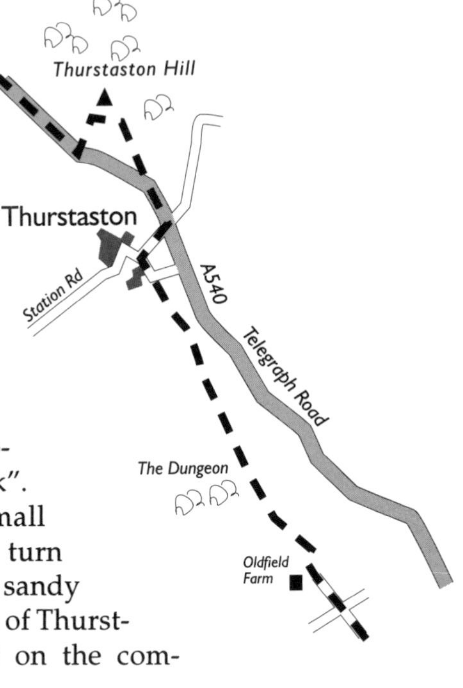

At the lane continue straight ahead and take the first road on the right beyond the church. Turn left at the busy A540 and bear right onto Thurstaston Common just beyond the Cottage Loaf public house, signposted "Public Footpath to Royden Park". Follow the path to a small school and just beyond, turn sharp left onto a broad sandy path which rises to the top of Thurstaston Hill, highest point on the common.

Chapter 5

Thurstaston to Hilbre Point

Distance: *5½ miles*

AT 255 feet, Thurstaston Hill is not the highest point in Wirral but it undoubtedly has one of the finest panoramas. A view finder near the highest point identifies major land marks along with distances and was erected in 1942 in memory of Andrew Blair, founder of Liverpool and District Ramblers Association. An inscription reads "For many years a keen worker for the preservation of cross country footpaths and amenities of the countryside. Author of several books for walkers."

The view on a clear day takes in much of Wirral and North Wales. Below us green fields sweep down from Thurstaston church to the marshes and shallow waters of the Dee Estuary, while the Clwydian Hills stand proudly beyond. If you are lucky the higher peaks of Snowdonia and the Great Orme will just be visible.

Thurstaston Hill

Further north the wooded slopes of Caldy Hill act as a barrier to the urban sprawl of eastern Wirral. Fields and woods quickly give way to houses, factories, pylons and motorways. Beyond is the familiar Liverpool skyline dominated by its two cathedrals.

The whole of Thurstaston Common was purchased by Birkenhead Town Council as far back as 1879 for "the benefit of the neighbourhood" and "convenience of the inhabitants". Had this not been the case, this bit of greenery may well have disappeared beneath the bricks and mortar of suburbia decades ago.

From the triangulation pillar descend to the car park immediately below the summit and turn right along the road. After about ½ mile turn left into fields where a sign indicates the "Public Footpath to Caldy". Keep to the field edge turning right through a gate in the corner and after a second field join a wide track which cuts through a horse paddock towards Caldy.

At the road continue straight ahead (Long Hey Road) and after 150 yards, where the road bears left, continue on the enclosed footpath (sign, "Public Footpath to Stapledon Wood"). Turn left at the road and continue towards Caldy village.

The Column

Look for a footpath sign on the right ("Public Bridleway") beside Caldecot Cottage and follow the sandy footpath into the woods. At the road turn left and then right into Thorsway. After about 150 yards cross over and take the enclosed footpath between gardens on the left. Turn right in the woods and at a clearing bear half-left by wooden seats in the direction of two distant masts. Continue now on the obvious footpath to the column at Column Road.

This was erected in 1841 by the Trustees of Liverpool Docks as a

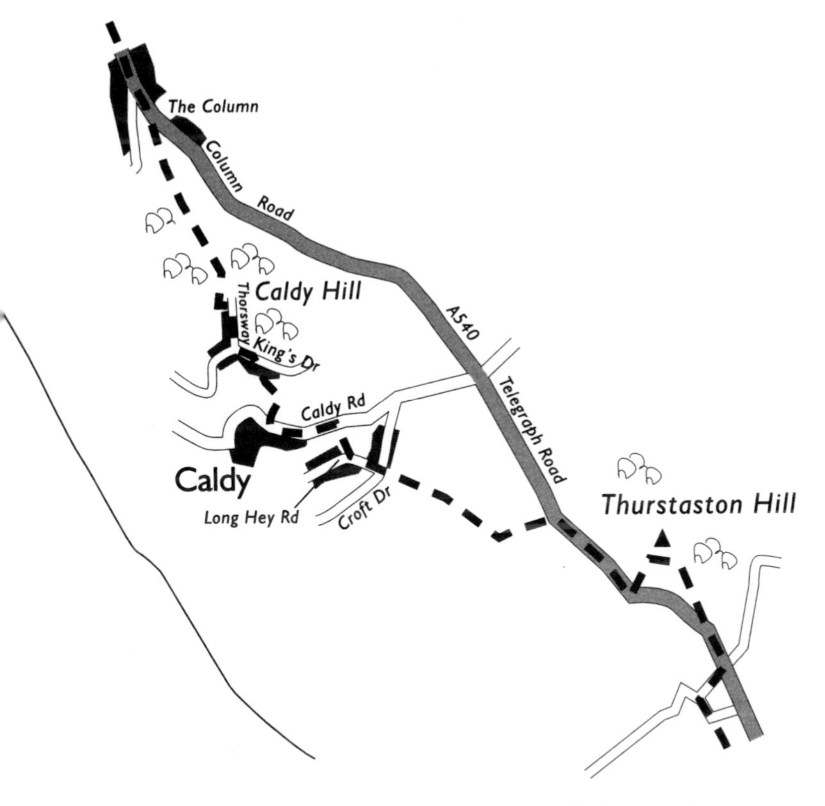

beacon for river traffic and replaced a large windmill destroyed two years earlier by gales which had also been used as a landmark by shipping.

Turn left into Column Road and where the road bears left down the hill, cross over and continue along Grange Old Road (beside Black House Hill). A well hidden footpath (sign "Public Footpath to Grange Hill") which joins the driveway to Grange Hill, a large house on the right, leads to the war memorial on the hill itself.

From the memorial continue northwards over the hill to Lang Lane and turn left. Follow the road to Redhouse Lane, a cul-de-sac on the right which eventually runs into a narrow footpath between gardens. At Orrysdale Road cross over and take a footpath on the left beside the school. Follow the path over the railway and straight across the following road onto a similar footpath. At the busy A540 (Meols Drive) turn right and after 300 yards bear left into Pinfold Lane. At the end of the lane continue straight across the golf course to the shoreline opposite Hilbre Island. Turn right now and either follow the sand or wooden walkway to Hilbre Point.

200 years ago this northern coast was a very different place. A line of shifting sand dunes battered by gales sheltered a handful of fishermen's

Hilbre Island

cottages, yet evidence of some of Wirral's earliest settlements have been found here. The finds, which include coins, brooches, precious stones and pottery, cover a period of 1,700 years and date back to the Roman outpost thought to have existed at Meols. Many of the items were recovered from the famous "submerged forest" visible on the sand at low tide until about 60 years ago. The late Norman Ellison in his book The Wirral Peninsula *describes the forest in this way: "The clean stretch of sand was broken by a black patch, perhaps a half-mile in length, which a closer inspection revealed to be a thick stratum of peat, brown twigs, leaves, mosses, ferns and lichens, all tightly compressed. Above this mass, a large number of tree trunks, perhaps three or four feet high, stood erect, whilst many fallen trunks and large branches lay partly buried."*

The origin of the forest is uncertain but it could well be a relic of Wirral's ancient woodland buried by shifting sands before deforestation could take place. Certainly this part of Wirral has seen dramatic changes in the last 700 years. The sand flats at nearby Hoylake were once a deep water pool or lake, known as "Hyle Lake", which existed until the canalisation of the Dee in the eighteenth century caused it to silt up.

It was referred to as the "Heyepol" during the reign of King John and was protected by a great sand bank which extended across the mouth of the estuary. It was used for centuries as a deep water anchorage and embarkation point by ships too large to reach Chester and it was from here that William III sailed to Ireland in 1690 to defeat James II at the Battle of the Boyne. Duke Schomberg gathered William's army of almost 10,000 here and sailed to Ireland in 90 ships which had anchored in Hoyle Lake.

When the lake finally disappeared it was replaced by a fine sandy beach which, during the nineteenth century when sea bathing became fashionable, attracted a large host of pleasure seekers eager to sample this new found pastime. Today Hoylake still has its sandy beach though you will find no sign of Hoyle Lake or the submerged forest.

Across the sand to the left lies Hilbre Island, easily reached at low tide and once home to a seventh century hermit by the name of Hidleburgh. There is no record of who this lady was or even how long she lived on Hilbre, but her solitary life of prayer and penance inspired the setting up of a holy shrine which attracted pilgrims throughout the Middle Ages.

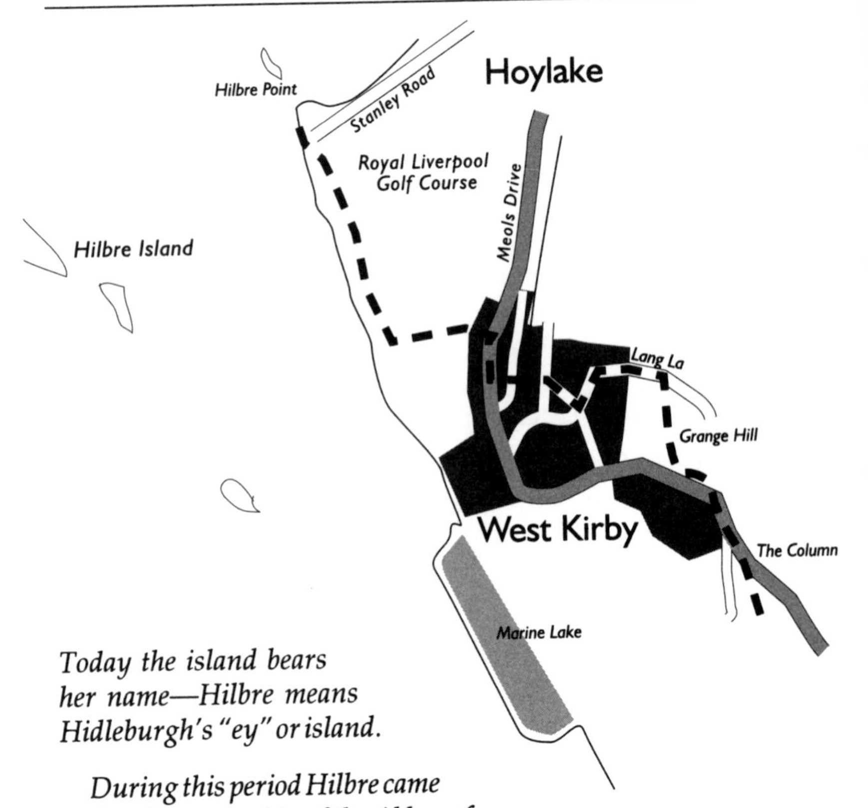

Today the island bears her name—Hilbre means Hidleburgh's "ey" or island.

During this period Hilbre came under the ownership of the Abbey of Saint Werburgh at Chester and monks in varying numbers lived on the island until the mid sixteenth century. By this time life was far from quiet in this busy corner of Wirral. As we have already learned, ships often used the nearby Hoyle Lake as an anchorage and as they grew in numbers a customs house was built and officers stationed here. Hilbre is also mentioned as the embarkation point for thousands of Queen Elizabeth's troops sent to conquer Ireland in the sixteenth century.

There has even been a small amount of industry on Hilbre. In 1662 an individual by the name of Dr Leigh set up a salthouse for the production of salt using raw materials brought from the mid Cheshire salt fields at Northwich. There has also been a public house although its owners are reputed to have gathered more wealth through the activity of wrecking.

Today the visitor will find little evidence of these activities although a trip across the sands makes a fine alternative finish to the Wirral Shore Way. You can reach the islands from the slipway at the northern end of the Marine Lake, West Kirby, about two hours either side of low water (the tide surrounds the islands for four hours out of every twelve). Aim for Little Eye, the southern most and smallest island, then follow the sandstone reef to Middle Eye and finally Hilbre Island.

Mara Publications

Mara Publications publish a range of walking books for Cheshire and North Wales and have the following list to date:

Cheshire

Circular Walks in Wirral

ISBN 0 9522409 1 2. A collection of 16 circular walks in the coast and countryside of Wirral.

Circular Walks along the Gritstone Trail and Mow Cop Trail

ISBN 0 9522409 4 7. A route which follows Cheshire's eastern border along the edge of the Peak District. Following the same format as the Sandstone Trail book—a full description for both trails is combined with 12 circular walks.

Circular Walks along the Sandstone Trail

ISBN 0 9522409 2 0. The Sandstone Trail is Cheshire's best known and most popular walking route. This book gives a complete route description along with 12 circular walks covering the entire trail.

North Wales

Coastal Walks around Anglesey (volume 1)

ISBN 0 9522409 6 3. A collection of 15 walks which explore the varied scenery of Anglesey's beautiful coastline.

Coastal Walks around Anglesey Volume 2

ISBN 0 9522409 5 5. A companion volume to the above book, outlining 15 new walks spread around Anglesey's fascinating and beautiful coastline.

Circular Walks in the Conwy Valley

ISBN 0 9522409 7 1. A collection of 15 circular walks which explore the varied scenery of this beautiful valley from the Great Orme to Betws-y-Coed.

Walking in the Clwydian Hills and the Vale of Llangollen

ISBN 0 9522409 3 9. A collection of 15 circular walks exploring the beautiful hills and valleys of the Welsh borders.

Circular walks along the Offa's Dyke Path—Volume 1 Prestatyn to Welshpool

ISBN 1 902512 01 4. The first volume in a series which will sample some of the finest sections of this well known national trail.

Walking on the Lleyn Peninsula

ISBN 1 902512 00 6. A collection of 16 circular walks which explore the wild and beautiful coastline and hills of the Lleyn Peninsula.

Local History

Picturesque Wirral

ISBN 0 9522409 9 8. A reprint of part of T.A. Coward's "Picturesque Cheshire" dealing with Wirral, originally published in 1903. A fascinating glimpse of Wirral in the closing years of the nineteenth century.

Picturesque Cheshire—Chester and the Welsh border

ISBN 1 902512 03 0. Like the above, this is a reprint of two chapters from T.A. Coward's "Picturesque Cheshire", originally published in 1903, dealing with the city of Chester and the western limits of the county bordering Wales. A fascinating glimpse of this historic city in the closing years of the nineteenth century.